Blasphemy, Banditry, Buraq-ery: A Poetry Chapbook

Ibrahim S. Amin

Published by Debonair Walrus, 2024.

BLASPHEMY, BANDITRY, BURAQ-ERY: A POETRY CHAPBOOK

First edition. April 5, 2024.

ISBN: 979-8224173877

Written by Ibrahim S. Amin.

Table of Contents

Introduction: The Wellspring of Atrocities...1

The Persian Woman...3

Mohammed Screams...5

Their Idol Burns..6

The Black Stone..8

Magic Carpets... 13

Beneath the Masjid... 15

Hyperspace Hajj.. 16

Mohammed.. 22

Jihadi Hijinks.. 24

Mo-Ho-Ho... 25

The Quran: An Abridged Trova Translation 31

About the Author 60

Introduction: The Wellspring of Atrocities

Islam's blasphemy codes cause harm on two levels.

First, we have the direct harm they inflict on accused blasphemers. In places such as Pakistan the legal system punishes them, as happened at the start of this month (March 2024) in Punjab Province, where a court sentenced a 22-year-old student to death and a 17-year-old to life imprisonment for allegedly sending blasphemous messages on WhatsApp. Islamic lunacy and brutality, enshrined in law. Though many Pakistani Muslim fanatics prefer to take injustice into their own hands rather than waiting for the courts, as happened on 16 August 2023 when a mob in Jaranwala burned down Christians' homes and churches because someone accused a Christian family of desecrating the Quran.

We see Islamic anti-blasphemy violence in the west too. On 12 August 2022, a jihadist terrorist repeatedly stabbed Salman Rushdie on stage in Chautauqua, New York, inflicting life-changing injuries and attempting to murder him for the 'crime' of writing *The Satanic Verses* decades earlier.

The second level of harm is less obvious but arguably even more damaging. Islam's blasphemy prohibitions prevent people from challenging, criticising, mocking, or denouncing Mohammed, the Quran, and the religion's orthodoxies. In other words, these prohibitions shield Islam itself. Muslim fundamentalists and supremacists commit countless atrocities across the world, whether it's the institutionalised marriage and rape of little girls in Afghanistan, the execution of gay men in Houthi-controlled Yemen, the persecution of Hindus in the Subcontinent, the massacre of Christians in Nigeria, or the large-scale rape and slaughter they inflicted on Israeli Jews, Bedouins, and guestworkers on 7 October 2023. They commit these atrocities because of Mohammed, the Quran, and the Hadith, then they wield blasphemy laws, violence, and the threat of violence to terrorise people into showing slavish deference to those same things that inspired and incited their atrocities in the first place.

Ending Islamic oppression and violence means undermining and dismantling Islam's central falsehoods. And to achieve that, we must normalise blasphemy.

The Persian Woman

Islamic rulers wield the knife,
They howl, "Immodesty is rife!
What sinful harlots you've become!
Our prophet damns you! Zina! Strife!"

The Persian woman won't succumb,
She burns hijabs, defies the scum,
She plucks a mullah from her hair
And crushes him beneath her thumb.

The others flee before her glare,
She sweeps her hand and swats a pair,
The Persian woman will not kneel,
No mullah tells her what to wear.

The revolution turns its wheel,
The woman's forged from Persian steel,
She plucks Mohammed from her life
And crushes him beneath her heel.

~~~~~

I have immense respect for the brave Iranians who challenge the tyranny of the Islamic Republic, especially women who walk in public without the hijab and thus defy the morality police and other Muslim fundamentalists. If they succeed in bringing down the regime and making Iran a post-Islamic country, the whole world benefits.
~~~~~

This interlocking rubaiyat's a Persian poetic form, and seemed appropriate for the subject matter.

Mohammed Screams

Mohammed screams in hell's domain,
He vomits ayats, blood, and pain,
"An infidel wreaks blasphemy,
He scuffs Qurans and tortures me!
Jihadists, help! I need him slain!"

Another tears Qurans in twain,
The prophet cries, "Jihad!" in vain,
In surahs spawned from agony,
Mohammed screams.

The kuffars shun Islamic reign,
And treat his lies with full disdain,
Ignoring every threat and plea,
They burn his scripture merrily;
Infernos blazing through his brain,
Mohammed screams.

~~~~~

I wrote this rondeau following an incident that happened at Kettlethorpe High School in Wakefield, here in the UK, during February 2023. A 14-year-old autistic boy brought a copy of the Quran to school, and caused minor scuff marks to its pages when he dropped it during some horseplay with his friends. This was his copy of the Quran, his own property. No one else's business. But local Muslim fundamentalists howled for vengeance, they sent the boy death threats, and the scuffing was reported to the police as a possible hate crime. The boy's mother had to go to the local mosque and apologise to the mob for her son's safety.
~~~~~

Their Idol Burns

"An angel spoke its holy words!"
They still believe Mohammed's jape
And tales of magic bomber birds;
The book which let Mohammed rape.

"Its surahs hold morality:
A Jew becomes a pig or ape!
Its verses, our reality."
The book which let Mohammed rape.

"Its ancient edicts rule our lives:
It banned the sweet fermented grape
And said instead to beat our wives!"
The book which let Mohammed rape.

"Respect the Prophet's sacred text!"
They scream with frothing mouths agape,
"Or else we'll slay your children next!"
The book which let Mohammed rape.

And yet Qurans will burn to ash,
Their false religion won't escape
But find its place among the trash;
The book which let Mohammed rape.

~~~~~

On 20 July 2023, a mob in Baghdad stormed the Swedish embassy as an act of revenge, because Sweden didn't prevent an Iraqi Christian from
~~~~~

protest-burning his own copy of the Quran. As with the Quran-scuffing incident that inspired the previous poem, the mindless fanatical fetishisation of the Quran was on full display. We'll come back to that subject later, in the author's note to the final poem in this chapbook.

When Islamic mobs and murderers punish blasphemy, the correct response is for all of us to blaspheme even more in defiance. Hence this kyrielle.

The refrain line ("The book which let Mohammed rape.") isn't random polemic. In Quran 33.50, which Mohammed preached as the supposed literal speech of Allah, he gave himself sexual rights to the infidel women he and his cultists had captured and enslaved. So, the Quran did quite literally let Mohammed rape. He was a sexual predator and made that one of the perks of his fraudulent prophethood.

The Black Stone

The ebon god draws power from their screams;
They throng the sand and jostle, screeching prayers
Towards a god who's aeons-dead but dreams,
And shudder at the form his idol wears.
Their plunder from a rival desert tribe
(It stood impassive, watched them kill and rape),
The secrets of its sculpting don't survive;
No living peoples carved its nightmare shape.
Their witches babble contradicting tales:
"Misshapen creatures born beneath the earth!"
"An island nation drowned among the whales!"
"The djinn and demons long before man's birth!"
No matter whence it came, they praise his might;
They offer sacrifices, day and night.

They offer sacrifices, day and night,
Maraud to pay the ebon god his due;
They slash their captives' guts for his delight,
They ululate and cheer the offal's spew.
The witches dream his whispers, speak his will:
"Consume their innards, taste the captives' doom;
Each pregnant woman must first gorge her fill
And glut the child who writhes inside her womb."
The ebon idol's shadow daubs their feasts,
Its darkness seethes within the churn of gore;
Their newborn children grow the teeth of beasts,
Become the horrors other tribes abhor.
Across the desert, rival priests convene,
Allianced by the carnage they have seen.

Allianced by the carnage they have seen,
A dozen hardy tribes amass that day;
Beneath the idol's ancient ebon sheen,
They fall upon the cannibals and slay.
The ebon god's devotees never yield;
Each howls and cleaves until their weapon breaks,
Then gouges, bites, and strews the battlefield
With eyes and tongues and dies in crimson lakes.
The allied tribesmen raise no victors' cheers
But toil in silence, cast their ropes, and heave;
The idol crashes down atop the smears;
They smash its nightmare likeness, spit, and leave.
By moonlight, hissing, creeping from a cave,
The beast-toothed children feast upon his grave.

The beast-toothed children feast upon his grave,
They swallow ebon splinters, howl, and bleed;
The weakest, dying, gibber, thrash and rave,
But stronger twisted hearts embrace his seed.
And through the generations it endures,
The splinters grow within descendants' hearts,
In dreaming death, the ebon god ensures
His era-spanning scheme shall have its parts.
But younger aeons' gods oppose his will:
Their servants hunt the splinter-bearers down,
Diminishing his cult with every kill
And thwarting his regaining of his crown
Until a single splinter still remains.
A magus seeks it out and walks the plains.

A magus seeks it out and walks the plains,

"An angel!" peasants say who see his face;
He smiles and hides the centuries of pains,
For though long-lived, he's no immortal race.
He's spilled his share of blood upon this world
And yearns to end his butchery at last;
A final kill and then the quest's unfurled;
He'll earn his grave and let his age be past.
The magus comes to Mecca, senses prey,
And flinches, for he finds an orphan boy
Whose cultist parents never lived to say
The ebon god will use him to destroy.
"I'll slay no innocent!" the magus cries;
His holy magic sparks within his eyes.

His holy magic sparks within his eyes,
He lays the boy within the deepest trance.
"The cursed ebon god won't have his prize!"
His hand becomes a glowing golden lance.
It splits the orphan's ribcage, spreading bone;
He plucks the ebon splinter from his breast,
Its evil burns the magus, makes him groan,
He hurls it, swears, and seals the orphan's chest.
The magus shakes, the deed has left him spent,
His death is near, he'll greet it with a grin;
His holy touch has cleansed the boy it rent,
Who'll wake upon his life absolved of sin.
The magus stumbles off, his vision blurred;
Mohammed wakes and wonders what occurred.

Mohammed wakes and wonders what occurred
But shrugs it off, returning to his game:
He laughs and throws a rock and hits a bird,

Then beats another child and mocks her name.
Mohammed grows, and learns to hide his crimes;
He smiles when merchants say, "An honest man!"
He's cheated every Meccan countless times;
A swindler's life remains his only plan.
But then he hears the whispers, and he heeds:
He finds the mountain cave and ventures in,
And there's the splinter, swollen by his deeds;
It offers twisted prophethood and sin.
Mohammed builds his cult; the Kaaba teems;
The ebon god draws power from their screams.

~~~~~

This crown of sonnets brings together different Islamic stories and blends them with fantasy and horror concepts from the early 20th century American pulps. The black stone of the Kaaba is a real thing, and there are various myths and legends about it. Present-day pilgrims try to kiss it when they circle the Kaaba during Hajj, which is quite remarkable if you consider how Islam rails against idol-worship.

There's an unrelated myth in Islam about how an angel or a pair of angels knocked Mohammed out when he was a boy, removed a black seed or sliver of sin from his heart, and washed his heart to purify it. In theological terms, Muslims believe this shows how heaven prepared him for his future prophethood. In narrative terms, it's just a way to embellish Mohammed and make his life seem more miraculous, like that of various other religious and mythological figures.

Pulp-wise, Robert E. Howard wrote a few different stories in which a black stone ties into eldritch horror of the sort people tend to associate with H. P. Lovecraft (himself a friend and correspondent of Howard's).
~~~~~

In the one actually entitled *The Black Stone* (1931), the eponymous stone's a pillar, whereas in the Bran Mak Morn story *Worms of the Earth* (1932) it's something more akin to Islam's Kaaba stone.

12

Magic Carpets

Islamic landmines detonate,
Exploding scriptures viscerate;
Reformists claim: "We'll solve it, mate!"

"Interpretation, that's the key!
Jihadists swagger lazily
In minefields, irresponsibly,
And trigger blasts of blood and hate."

"They simply need to reassess;
Our dissonance will fix this mess:
Delusions spun as faithfulness;
We'll show the world Mohammed's great!"

"A passage claims he raped a kid?
And people copy what he did?
An irksome mine, and better hid...
We'll carpet over Aisha's fate!"

"A verse denouncing Jews as thieves?
The word of God, Islam believes;
Another mine our scripture leaves!
We'll lay a carpet, set them straight!"

"Disarm the mines? It can't be done!
Accept Mohammed lied for fun?
That's heresy! The stuff we shun!
I'm sure our rugs will bear the weight..."

~~~~~

It's been nearly a decade since I left Islam, and over that time I've come to realise how inherently flawed almost all Islamic reform actually is. These so-called reforms largely just involve intellectual and textual gymnastics and cognitive dissonance designed to make Islam look good in front of a non-Muslim audience or else make a moderate Muslim feel better about their personal beliefs by clumsily back-projecting them onto Mohammed and the Quran. The problem is, this approach has no wider effectiveness. You can talk about "interpretation" all you want, and pretend the Quran and Hadith don't really support all the terrible things they proclaim, but a more devout or intellectually honest Muslim will simply look at the text itself and see you're wrong.

Even if you do somehow succeed in persuading a few other Muslims to adopt your sanitised interpretation of scripture, and carpet over the landmines, those landmines remain there, ready to blow people up down the line. We saw this in the Islamic revolutions of the 20th century, when more liberal Islamic societies in places like Egypt, Iran, and Afghanistan fell back beneath the tyranny of orthodox Islamic belief and its consequences.

Moreover, human rights such as the right of little girls to be safe from paedophilic marriage and rape shouldn't ever rely on how Muslims arbitrarily interpret scripture. Instead, those rights should trump Mohammed, the Quran, and all their teachings and interpretations.

Instead of interpretation, instead of cognitive dissonance and carpets over landmines, real reform means accepting the Quran's a man-made text and that Mohammed said and did bad things rather than being any kind of role model for mankind.
~~~~~

Beneath the Masjid

They raze the temple, lay their stones
And build a masjid, grind the bones
Of ancient gods; their mullah drones:
"A temple? Never here."

His sermons name invaders brave
And celebrate the mosque they gave;
A murder victim's shallow grave.
"No god but Allah here!"

By day, the worship hides the sound;
At night, it whispers underground;
He prays the body won't be found.
"May Allah hide our crime!"

~~~~~

During the Islamic invasion of India, temples fell and mosques rose on their sites, in the name of Mohammed and Islam's hatred of polytheism and idols. The rebuilding of temples in present-day India sometimes gets framed as a provocation, but in many ways it's an act of decolonisation.
~~~~~

Hyperspace Hajj

Saffiya woke from hypersleep;
Emerging from her stasis pod,
She flinched beneath the warning bleep.

Computer blared: "Affront to God!
Securing door! Conceal your hair!
Remember: You're a mixed-sex squad!"

Hijab dispensers joined the blare
And blasted fabric, made her spin;
"Remember: Allah's everywhere!"

Saffiya hid her hair within
The flying cloth, she wrapped it tight.
A chime declared her free of sin.

Within the bridge's garish light,
Saffiya took her console, gazed;
She'd dreamed this through galactic night.

Her captain shouted, "God be praised!
The Prophet's missing world is found!
We'll resurrect what fools erased!"

"Descend to Mecca's sacred ground,"
He ordered Saff, "without delay!
The Kaaba beckons, circle round!"

"Electric storms impede our way."

She pointed. "They'd destroy the ship."
"We'll walk those miles. It's Hajj today!"

They landed past the lightning's whip
And suited-up, with guns and gear.
Computer flashed a warning blip.

"Alert!" it said. "Menstruation smear!"
Saffiya winced and Zara cried:
"I have to go! The Kaaba's near!"

The captain chided, "Sinful pride!
You'd desecrate Mohammed's shrine?
Uncleanliness! You'll stay inside!"

"I must do Hajj! The honour's mine!"
And Zara shoved him, made a break.
He drew his blaster, shot her spine.

"The rest of you, I'll deign to take."
He gestured. "But avoid her gore;
Remain unstained for Allah's sake!"

They dodged the corpse and bloody floor;
Men cursed at Zara's treachery:
"Mohammed damn that filthy whore!"

Saffiya whispered, "May it be
That Allah hears my pilgrim prayer,
Redeeming her Islamically."

They trod upon the glassy layer
Of nuclear weapons' ancient rage,
Beneath the djinn-like storming air.

"Along here, in Mohammed's age..."
The ship's imam informed the crew
And climbed a hill. "...upon this stage..."

"...a battle... Wait. You hear that too?"
A creature hurtled from the skies
And gleaming feathers ripped him through.

It landed, screeching fearsome cries
Amid the sweep of metal wings:
A mule with human face and eyes.

"Buraq!" Saffiya knew the things
That Cybertollahs wrought to clash
But slaughtered those who held their strings.

"Detected: Wretched Sunni trash!"
A crewman yelled, "I'm Shia though!"
It disembowelled him with a slash.

A woman crunched beneath its blow;
The captain raged, his weapon blazed:
"We'll lay this Shia idol low!"

The shards of metal feathers grazed
Saffiya's visor, scarred the world;
The bursts of blasters left her dazed.

The robot's sparking wing unfurled,
The captain's gunfire shredded it;
Saffiya screamed for God and hurled.

Her vision blurred, grenade still hit:
Its head exploded, shards and sludge;
The captain grunted. "Shia shit."

They left their dead, said, "God will judge!"
And trekked upon the path they took
In search of martyrdom or Hajj.

The captain yelled, "The Kaaba! Look!"
Its ruined masjid rose ahead;
And from its rubble, war cries shook.

Saffiya reeled; the world was dead,
A ruin countless wars had made!
She swore at what its carcass bred.

The Meccan mutants charged and brayed,
A twisted horde, monstrosities,
With broken tech reused as blade.

Saffiya said, "We're pilgrims! Please!"
A howling mutant swung a sword
With peeling ancient script; Chinese?

She dodged and shot, Saffiya roared;
The captain joined her, back-to-back

They reaped the frothing mutant horde.

They stumbled from the last attack,
Just two upon a corpse-strewn hell.
She trod on bone and fled the crack.

They knelt before the Kaaba's shell,
And something glittered, black as night:
Mohammed's stone survived as well.

Saffiya laughed her mad delight:
"We'll take it from this ruined place
And build New Mecca, make this right!"

"A Hajj," she said, "in settled space,
For generations yet to be!"
Her pious visions warmed her face.

The captain bellowed, "Heresy!"
He fired; Saffiya's innards burned.
"Mohammed's land! Eternity!"

Saffiya slumped, the red sky churned,
And he performed the Hajj he'd earned.

~~~~~

I'm more of a fantasy writer than a sci-fi writer, but there's something satisfying about sci-fi's ability to project ideas into the far future and explore the mindsets and societies they'd create, whether it's the Nazi-won future of Katharine Burdekin's *Swastika Night* (1937), the engineered humanity of Aldous Huxley's *Brave New World* (1932), or
~~~~~

the book-burning society of Ray Bradbury's *Fahrenheit 451* (1953). We don't get all that much sci-fi which deconstructs Islamic ideas via this sort of projection, other than maybe the galactic jihad of the *Dune* novels (1965-85 for Frank Herbert's original six-book series), so I figured I'd give it a shot.

Mohammed

"Allah's sent a message!" said Mohammed.
"Prophet cutbacks! Laid off!" read Mohammed.

Snatching choicest women, claimed as plunder,
Homeward bound to rape them fled Mohammed.

Aisha played with dolls like other children;
Childhood ruined, made to wed Mohammed.

Wives with throbbing bruises curse his verses,
Secretly; they know to dread Mohammed.

Zaynab, Jewish heroine of Khaybar,
Poisoned lamb and then she fed Mohammed.

Muslims claim the Temple Mount, declaring:
"From this place to heaven sped Mohammed!"

"Camel piss will nourish!" claimed the prophet.
Jesus sighed. "Just give them bread, Mohammed."

Booksellers destroy Quranic surplus;
Mobs say, "Kuffar scum! They shred Mohammed!"

Other cultures dream up better heroes;
Muslims kiss the bones of dead Mohammed.

~~~~~
~~~~~

The ghazal's an interesting poetic form, and I like how you end up with those free-standing couplets, telling their own little stories but united by the shared rhyme and repeated word(s) that appear at the ends of both lines of the first couplet and the second lines of the subsequent couplets.

Jihadi Hijinks

Abdul's mad!
He'll do jihad!
But, pious lad,
He thinks it bad
To skip a prayer.
The mosque is there...
In bomber-wear,
And lacking care,
He bows with flair.
The trigger? Hair!
Explosion's blare
And fiery glare
Everywhere!
Shatters panes
And scatters stains
Of Abdul's brains.

~~~~~

Skeltonic or tumbling verse may not be ideal for longer, more serious narrative poems, but I think it works pretty well for this sort of mad jihad-themed humour.
~~~~~

Mo-Ho-Ho

Mohammed trudged among the damned
And grumbled, pissed, for hell was crammed
With joyful demons, revelling.
He yelled, "Haram, the shit you sing!
A Christmas carol!?! Where's your pride,
To celebrate the twat who died
Upon his cross? (I hope it hurt
And made his Jewish innards squirt!)
It's bad enough they celebrate
Upon the Earth! I fucking hate
To hear the infidels rejoice,
But here in hell? You have no choice:
Reject the Nazarean scum!
A Christmas party? Fucking dumb!
You sinners should be cursing him!
You demons too, he made you swim
In lakes of lava—" "Actually,"
A teacher chided, "Mo, you see,
It's magma when it's underground..."
Mohammed made a snorting sound.
A fiend of gluttony opined:
"His birthday sees us wined and dined!
Eternal torment's quite the chore;
This Yule I'll eat my weight or more
In turkey, stuffing, brussel sprouts,
And drink a lake or thereabouts!"
A succubus said, "Stealing souls,
Seducing hard to hit my goals,
And stomping sinners' cocks to goo?
I need a little me-time too!

A chance to drink and sing and dance!
Don't mope, you jerk! Give fun a chance!"
The fiends and sinners echoed her,
Infernal prince to larcener.
Mohammed shunned them, traipsed away,
And vowed to ruin Christmas Day.

"But how?" he mused. "I... What's that noise?
That merry jingle? It annoys!
A jolly laugh, a chiming bell?
It's Santa Claus! He's come to hell!"
And sure enough, a sleigh flew past;
Mohammed chased, it dropped at last;
The reindeer landed, clattering,
Their magic hoofbeats scattering
A hundred swirling hellfire sparks,
Evoking triple-headed barks;
The runners sliced and smeared the ash,
And skidded hard to end the dash
In front of Satan's citadel,
The grandest house in all of hell.
"It's Nick!" said Satan, strolling forth,
"My cousin from the frozen north!
You've gained a heap of weight, you slob:
A scarlet sumo-wrestling blob!"
And Santa rolled out from his sleigh
And chuckled, "How's aboot you, eh?
You dipped your nose in fallen snow
Or snorted half a ton of blow?
The abs are nice, I'll give you that...
With heroin you don't get fat!"
They laughed, embraced, exchanging gifts:

A sword for Satan, several fifths
Of moonshine straight from heaven's still;
For Santa's magic sleigh, a grill
That blazed his name in gems and gold
From hell's own mines, their worth untold.
Then Satan beckoned him inside:
"We'll quaff and feast before you ride!"
They vanished through the castle gate;
Mohammed cheered this twist of fate.

He leapt in Santa's magic sleigh
And nudged the sack of gifts away.
"You reindeer better fucking fly..."
He drew his knife. "...or else you die!
I'll cut your throats, halal you up,
And chuck your guts to Satan's pup!"
The reindeer ran and rose and flew,
Inferno opened, let them through.
Mohammed whooped to see the stars;
"This Christmas Eve is mine, kuffaars!"
A festive market teemed below
With mulled wine, artificial snow,
A Christmas tree and webs of lights,
A manger scene and other sights.
Mohammed glowered; "Fuck is this?
That Jewish bastard's birth brings bliss!?!"
He reached in Santa's magic sack
And conjured weapons, howled, "Attack!"
He lobbed jihadist bomber vests,
Explosions shredded limbs and chests.
Mohammed made the reindeer swoop
And swing around the nearest group

Of screaming parents, children too,
He drew a sword and hacked them through
Their necks and sent their heads aflight
And cackled, "Yeah! Too fucking right!
You infidels forgot my way!?!"
He smashed a girl beneath the sleigh.
He soared and found a perfect spot
To land and watch the dying rot:
A church's roof; he kicked the cross.
"Begone, you piece of Christian dross!"
It fell and crushed a little boy;
Mohammed ululated joy.
He turned to fetch the magic sack;
"Jihad is tiring. Need a snack..."

"Mohammed!" came a voice on high;
A golden light bisected sky
And hosts of angels sang a song.
"Did hell not teach you right from wrong?"
And Jesus landed on the roof
And glared; Mohammed sneered, aloof:
"I wondered if you had the balls
To heed the shrieking losers' calls."
"How dare you walk upon the Earth
And slaughter those who praise my birth?
Repent, you fool, or else be smote!"
"Go fuck yourself and fuck a goat!"
So Jesus drew his golden blade,
Said, "Very well. The choice is made."
Mohammed met him, steel on steel,
His slashes made poor Jesus reel.
"I've slain a hundred Jews like you

And raped an equal number too!
In life you preached and gave out fish;
I bet you now begin to wish
You'd lived like me, the warlike way!"
He knocked him back against the sleigh
And Jesus bled and tripped and sprawled.
Mohammed waved his sword and called:
"Behold, you angels, watch his doom
And find his corpse an empty tomb!"
"Mohammed..." Jesus raised his hand.
"Your final chance, you understand?
Repent and lay your sword aside."
"I'll flay your fucking Jewish hide!"
He moved to strike and Jesus roared:
"You're right, I never led a horde!
At feats of arms, I'm not so great...
But I can transubstantiate!"
He turned Mohammed's blood to booze
And staggered up and cried, "You lose!"
Mohammed gurgled, frothed, and fell,
And Jesus sent him back to hell.

The demons had their holiday
And also made Mohammed pay:
They draped his guts around the tree;
He howled, "You're doing blasphemy!"
A succubus castrated him
Upon a merry Christmas whim;
She waved his bits while carolling
And laughed, "Mohammed, join me! Sing!"
He screeched in deepest agony;
She trilled along in harmony.

<div align="center">~~~~~</div>

Unless you happen to be reading this chapbook in December, it's probably not an ideal time for a Mohammed Christmas special. But the story popped into my head, so I ran with it.

The Quran: An Abridged Trova Translation

Surah 1: The Opening

Praising Allah! What a guy!
(Strange, because this book's his speech,
Yet he's in third person. Why?
"Just accept!" fanatics screech.)

Surah 2: The Cow

Don't like fighting, so you say?
Man up, wanker! Grab a sword!
Allah's bidding: slash and slay!
Pious Muslims, go maraud!

Surah 3: The Family of Imran

Imran's wife here gets no name,
Like all women, save her child:
Mary, she of Gospel fame;
Named to drive the kuffar wild!

Surah 4: Women

Beat a wife who's uppity;
Thump a bitch who misbehaves!
Don't commit adultery,
Save with married kuffar slaves.

Surah 5: The Food

In the cradle, Jesus spoke,
Then he made a bird of clay;
Brought the thing to life, no joke!
(Cribbed from Christian legends? Nay!)

Surah 6: The Cattle

Allah's God, and him alone!
Polytheists? Fucking trash!
Makes him rage upon his throne;
Change your ways, or Allah smash!

Surah 7: The Elevated Places

Homosexuality!?!
Men with men!?! Abhorrent sin!
Allah rained his doom on thee!
Lust for women, then you'll win.

Surah 8: The Spoils of War

So you robbed the infidel?
Awesome work! But pay your due,
Lest you want to burn in hell:
It belongs to Mo, not you!

Surah 9: Repentance

Jews call Ezra Allah's son.
Lying? Nah! I swear they do!
Not traducing them for fun;
Allah's word is always true.

Surah 10: Jonah

Think this revelation's fake?
Write a surah of your own!
Allah mocks the trash you make;
Epic rhymes are his alone!

Surah 11: Hud

Flooded world, the sinners died.
Noah though, he built a boat;
Fit a fucking zoo inside!
("Like a TARDIS." — Scholar's note)

Surah 12: Joseph

Mo deploys a Jewish tale,
Saying, "Revelation! Yeah!
Proves my propheting won't fail;
Doubting wankers, walk with care!"

Surah 13: The Thunder

Allah smites with thunderbolts,
Just like Zeus except for real.
Better though, his bolt exalts:

Hymns ring out in thunder's peal!

Surah 14: Abraham

Allah sends some folk astray,
Like a trickster deity.
(And this douchey stuff, they say,
Passes for morality?)

Surah 15: The Rock

God said, "Angels, bow to man;
Give my work a good review!"
Satan ruined Allah's plan,
Told him, "Bow? Ha! No! Fuck you!"

Surah 16: The Bee

Earthquakes? Allah's solved that flaw:
Mountains pin and hold the ground.
(Seems legit tectonic lore;
Scripture's science sure is sound...)

Surah 17: The Israelites

Giving scripture piece by piece,
Episodic, not to binge;
Revelations never cease!
(Lest Mohammed's people winge.)

Surah 18: The Cave

Alexander's Allah's mate,
Even though he worshipped Zeus.
(Allah's knowledge? Not so great.
Treats his history fast and loose.)

Surah 19: Mary

Mary groaned with labour pain.
Allah shrugged, a useless male;
Gave her dates, said, "Push again?"
(That's omnipotence!?! A fail!)

Surah 20: Ta Ha

Adam's named but Eve is not;
Sexist writing, through and through!
Else Mohammed just forgot
Women have their stories too.

Surah 21: The Prophets

Doubters say Mohammed lies;
Call him poet, fraud, deranged.
Countering, Mohammed tries
Claiming it's all prearranged.

Surah 22: The Pilgrimage

Disbelievers, that's not yours:
Abraham, he built that shrine!

Sure this story has some flaws,
Still, piss off, the Kaaba's mine!

Surah 23: The Believers

Pious menfolk, watch those cocks:
Only shag your wives and slaves!
Raping captured women rocks;
Willing girlfriends? Don't be knaves!

Surah 24: The Light

Tell your bitches, "Drop your gaze!
Going out? Hijab-up then!"
(Allah's scripture never says
Stuff to women, only men.)

Surah 25: The Criterion

Disbelievers questioning?
Calling out Mohammed's claims?
Brimstone preaching's just the thing!
Terrorise them! Threaten flames!

Surah 26: The Poets

Poets spreading disbelief,
Leading honest folk astray!
(Author's note, I'll keep it brief:
Who asked Allah anyway?)

Surah 27: The Ant

Solomon amassed his hosts:
Djinn and birds, he knew their speech!
(Prophet Mo? He only boasts
Common raiders, rapists each.)

Surah 28: The Narrative

Supervillains form a team.
Haman, Pharaoh: hardened heart!
Must have been a time-warp scheme;
Two men centuries apart.

Surah 29: The Spider

Idol-worship makes God mad;
Do it and he'll fuck you up.
Being gay? That's also bad!
Sipping from a sinful cup!

Surah 30: The Romans

Romans got their arses kicked;
Filthy pagans won the fight.
But the Romans won't stay licked;
Worship God, he'll grant you might!

Surah 31: Lukman

Allah built the universe;

Show me what your gods have made!
Worship him or face his curse!
(Or Mohammed's bloody blade.)

Surah 32: The Adoration

Allah wished to fill up hell,
Else he could've guided all.
Sinful humans, djinn as well;
Allah shrugged and let them fall.

Surah 33: The Allies

Mo has needs like other men.
Captive women? They're his prey!
Dinner guests should piss off when
Mo desires to rape away.

Surah 34: Sheba

Call Mohammed mad!?! You'll see!
(Seems like quite a common theme.)
Follow him and worship me!
(Clearly they saw through his scheme.)

Surah 35: The Creator

Allah threatens genocide,
Says he could just start afresh:
Wipe out humans, once his pride,
Sculpt replacement species' flesh.

Surah 36: Ya Sin

All-wise Allah says the sun
Sinks within a resting place.
(Don't you ruin Allah's fun,
Throwing physics in his face!)

Surah 37: The Rangers

Angels throng the conference room;
Sneaky djinn are eavesdropping;
Heavenly defences zoom:
Shooting stars that pelt and sting.

Surah 38: Sad

Naming guys from Hebrew lore,
Citing tales the hearers know:
Noah, Job, and several more.
(Stealing Judaism. Low!)

Surah 39: The Companies

Intercession? Not a chance!
God alone will damn or save!
(Islam's inconsistent stance:
Claims Mo helps beyond the grave.)

Surah 40: The Forgiving One

Angels carry Allah's throne,
Others sing a symphony,
Hymning for their God alone;
His bar mitzvah revelry!

Surah 41: Revelations Well Expounded

Body horror! Tales of hell:
Skin will speak and testify,
And your eyes, and ears as well;
Snitch upon you when you die.

Surah 42: The Counsel

Your misfortune? Allah's work;
Surely he must think you suck.
Makes some women barren (jerk!),
Rigs the game of life, not luck.

Surah 43: The Embellishment

Angels? Allah's daughters!?! No!
God denies paternity!
(Child support for hosts would blow;
Bankrupt for eternity!)

Surah 44: The Evident Smoke

Smoke emerges from the sky,
Tortures those who disbelieve.
Muslims revel when they die,

Shagging houris they receive.

Surah 45: The Kneeling

Allah names sharia here,
Says he laid it out for Mo.
(Nowhere else will it appear.
What a shitty cameo.)

Surah 46: The Sandhills

Djinn convert to Islam now,
Having heard Mohammed's law.
(Raises questions, such as how
Djinn don't know of God before.)

Surah 47: Muhammad

Smite the disbelievers' necks!
Have no fear, for death's your friend:
Muslims cash a martyr's cheques;
Wine in rivers greets your end!

Surah 48: The Victory

Allah's raids are lucrative:
Infidels have lots of loot;
Go to war and God will give!
Fail to fight? You get the boot!

Surah 49: The Chambers

Stop your shouting! Pack it in!
Prophet Mo deserves some chill!
If his words won't quell the din,
Allah's revelation will.

Surah 50: Qaf

Allah's omnipresent but
Lazy, thus he hires a crew:
Tracking all your sins and smut,
Pairs of angels follow you.

Surah 51: The Scatterers

Allah made the djinn and man
Only so they'd worship him!
(Pretty narcissistic plan;
Quite the supervillain's whim.)

Surah 52: The Mountain

More of heaven, more of hell,
(Repetition makes things stick!)
Once again, let Allah tell:
Houris will delight your dick!

Surah 53: The Star

Knock it off, you pagan twat;
Don't repurpose goddesses!

Allah's ego rails at that,
All of heaven's only his.

Surah 54: The Moon

Crack! The moon is split in twain;
(Astrophysics takes a knock...)
Heralds Judgement Day and pain;
Mess with us, we'll stomp your cock!

Surah 55: The Merciful

Dabbling with his poetry,
Allah fashions a refrain.
(Poets love that stuff, you see;
Copy-paste again, again.)

Surah 56: That Which Is Coming

Heaven's whores! We've mentioned those;
Worship Allah, shag his girls!
And for paederasts, suppose...
Pretty serving boys like pearls!

Surah 57: The Iron

Bored of Bronze Age loser tech,
God revealed the Iron Age:
Better blades to cleave a neck;
Slaughter-science turned a page.

Surah 58: She Who Pleaded

Allah hates the infidel;
He demands you hate them too!
That applies to kin as well;
Otherwise he'll batter you!

Surah 59: The Exile

Mo expelled a Jewish tribe
Like a Nazi piece of shit;
Allah cheers and makes a jibe.
(Pretty racist, you'll admit.)

Surah 60: She Who Is Tested

Shun the people Allah hates
And wives who apostatise.
Convert-women, take as mates;
Test them for their faith though, guys!

Surah 61: The Ranks

Jesus told them Mo would come!
(Didn't make the Gospels, though...)
Fight beside him, don't succumb!
(Would Jesus raid? Surely, no?)

Surah 62: The Day of Congregation

Talking shit about the Jews,

Smearing them with talk of sin.
Friday praying: run, don't snooze;
Judenfreitag feeling! Win!

Surah 63: The Hypocrites

Hypocrites! Their faith is fake!
We despise that wretched horde!
(Quite a brazen line to take,
For Mohammed was a fraud.)

Surah 64: The Cheating

Shun the earthly things you like:
Wealth and even children too;
Favour Allah's coming reich!
Sinful wives may feud with you.

Surah 65: The Divorce

Wed a prepubescent kid?
Yeah, that falls within the rules.
Can divorce them too; be rid,
If your child-brides act like fools.

Surah 66: The Prohibition

Allah handles Mo's affairs:
Says to break his oaths to wives,
Shagging new ones when he cares.
(Great disdain for women's lives.)

Surah 67: The Kingdom

Astral lamps, you call them stars:
Made to pelt demonic foes!
(Science launches probes to Mars;
Trumps the nonsense Allah 'knows'.)

Surah 68: The Pen

Say Mohammed's mad? The jerks!
Sure, he claims to hear a voice
Choosing him for God's own works...
But they'll burn and he'll rejoice!

Surah 69: The Inevitable

Judgement Day! The heavens tear
And the mountains grind to grit;
Angels carry Allah's chair.
(What a lazy fucking shit!)

Surah 70: The Ladders

Climb to heaven, grab a rung!
(Allah's God of Ladders too.)
Sinners, though, will fall unsung,
Ladders kicked from under you.

Surah 71: Noah

Allah made the moon a light!
(False! The moon reflects the sun,
Though its silver brings delight.
Allah: zero. Physics: one.)

Surah 72: The Jinn

Genies vary, some are bros
Who embrace Islamic truth;
Heaven grants them magic hoes!
Kuffar genies? They're uncouth!

Surah 73: The Mantled One

Sleep's for losers! Stay awake:
Chant Quranic verse by dark;
Worship hard for Allah's sake!
(Sleepless cultists? What a lark.)

Surah 74: The Clothed One

Nineteen angels guarding hell;
Ask me why that number's set...
Done to thwart the infidel.
(Prophet Mo was drunk, I bet.)

Surah 75: The Resurrection

Allah's necromancy's sound:
He'll assemble all your bones;
Dig your fingers from the ground,

Build your eyes new rods and cones.

Surah 76: The Man

Advertising paradise!
Did we mention handsome boys?
Serving cocktails; pretty nice!
Follow Allah, earn these joys!

Surah 77: The Emissaries

Judgement Day is coming, jerks!
Doom if you repudiate
Prophet Mo's authentic works
And deny he's Allah's mate.

Surah 78: The Tidings

Infidels will writhe in flame;
Boiling water's all they drink.
Muslims shag in Allah's name;
Heaven's magic houris blink.

Surah 79: Those Who Pull Out

More repeated greatest hits:
Trumpets sound for Judgement Day.
Moses gets on Pharaoh's tits.
Paradise: the faithful's pay.

Surah 80: He Frowned

(Judgement Day's a racist sight.)
Sinners' faces turn to black
While the pious shine as white.
(Allah should take this one back.)

Surah 81: The Cessation

End times! Portents filled with dooms:
Every single star will fall!
(Stars aren't lamps that hang in rooms;
Did God go to school at all?)

Surah 82: The Cleaving Asunder

More apocalyptic signs:
Planets scattered, seas poured out;
Part of Allah's grand designs!
(Terrorising the devout.)

Surah 83: The Defrauders

Hell and heaven beckoning.
Muslims get the final laugh:
Lounge on couches, tittering,
Watching sinners shriek and barf.

Surah 84: The Rending

More apocalyptic lore:
Earth is emptied, lives are weighed.

(Frankly, Allah's quite the bore;
Should revise this book he's made.)

Surah 85: The Constellations

Allah punishes the crime:
Persecute believers? Die!
(Mo can pillage any time;
Admonitions don't apply.)

Surah 86: The Night-Comer

Allah style biology:
Semen gushes from a spot
Twixt the ribs and loins, you see!
(Educated, Allah's not.)

Surah 87: The Most High

Allah helps Mohammed learn;
Mo forgets what Allah deigns.
(Verses Allah wants to burn?
Mo's excuse if memory wanes?)

Surah 88: The Overwhelming Calamity

Camels prove that Allah's true:
Look at them, their awesome humps!
Evolution couldn't do
Anything that awesome, chumps.

Surah 89: The Dawn

Allah's ravaged countless folk,
Smashing them for evil deeds;
Mess with him and you'll be broke!
(Threats so Mo gets what he needs.)

Surah 90: The City

Fire's your awning when in hell!
(Flaming ceilings? That seems new.
Nice that Allah knows to tell
Many tales to threaten you.)

Surah 91: The Sun

Allah wrecked Thamud, a tribe,
Punishing their blasphemy.
(Pretty much the standard vibe;
Allah lacks variety.)

Surah 92: The Night

Wealth won't save you from the fires;
Charity? Now, that delights!
(Later verses, it transpires,
Grant Mohammed plunder rights.)

Surah 93: The Early Hours

God tells Mo that he's his bro:

Allah's always got his back.
(Prophet Mo composed this though;
Narcissistic maniac!)

Surah 94: The Expansion

Allah takes your burdens off;
Toil and strive and give him more:
Take on burdens he can doff!
(That's a scam, I'm pretty sure.)

Surah 95: The Fig

Allah swears by olives, figs:
"Shaped you from the greatest clay;
Then I made you total pigs,
Save for those who kneel and pray!"

Surah 96: The Clot

Made man from a bloody clot,
Like an evil scientist;
Sin against God? Better not,
Lest he grab your forelock, twist!

Surah 97: The Majesty

Better than a hundred years:
Night of Power, bonus prayers;
Christmas for Mohammed's peers!
(But no presents, so who cares?)

Surah 98: The Proof

Worst of creatures? Infidels!
Pagan, Jew, and Christian scum
Disbelieve what Allah tells;
Burn in hell for being dumb!

Surah 99: The Shaking

Mighty earthquakes shake the world,
Marking God's apocalypse;
Man will hear his sins unfurled
From the Earth's own magic lips!

Surah 100: The Assaulters

Man's ungrateful, like a horse,
Batters people, takes their pay!
(Muslims do the same, of course.)
Zombies rise on Judgement Day.

Surah 101: The Terrible Calamity

Fear apocalyptic doom:
Mountains getting fluffed apart;
Carded wool upon the loom!
Fire will burn a sinner's heart!

Surah 102: Worldly Gain

Out there seeking wealth today?
Allah scorns pursuing gain!
(How about Mohammed's play:
Feigning prophethood to reign?)

Surah 103: Time

Man is lost without good deeds!
(Super short, this surah here;
Any fortune cookie reads
Better, wiser; greater cheer.)

Surah 104: The Slanderer

Slander us? You'll burn in hell!
Wealth won't save you from that fate.
Libel lawyers burn as well;
Don't defend a man I hate!

Surah 105: The Elephant

Allah sent his bomber birds,
Dropping missiles baked from clay,
Killed the strategising nerds;
Elephant was air-raid prey.

Surah 106: The Quraish

Allah made your tribe the best,
Gave you caravans and wealth;
Praise his name with your whole chest:

God of economic health!

Surah 107: The Daily Necessaries

People who reject our spiel
Hate the orphans, hate the poor,
Pray for show and not for real;
All the stuff that we abhor!

Surah 108: Abundance

Allah gave you everything;
Thank him, pray, and sacrifice.
Unbelievers? They lack bling;
Their posterity's not nice!

Surah 109: The Unbelievers

Disbelievers? Keep your gods!
Allah's better; we won't quit!
You and we shall be at odds:
We have truth and you have shit!

Surah 110: The Help

Everyone will come to God!
Trust me, bro, and get in first.
Don't be late, a wretched sod;
Snag the best seat, not the worst!

Surah 111: The Flame

Abu Lahab? Piece of shit!
Allah hates him, just like me,
And he'll burn that irksome twit,
Fuck his wife up too, you'll see!

Surah 112: The Unity

Allah has no mum or dad
And he didn't have a kid.
Christmas dinner's rather sad;
Probably makes him wish he did.

Surah 113: The Daybreak

Darkness! Evil! Witchery!
Allah made them; kind of weird;
Quite unnecessarily,
Crafted all the things you've feared.

Surah 114: The Men

Trust in Allah, he's your king
And your God: remember that!
Though it seems a funny thing
Only Satan wants to chat...

~~~~~

The Quran's a terrible book, even if we set aside all the horrible things it
preaches, all the antisemitism, homophobia, misogyny, robbery, slavery,
rape, and slaughter. I've read a fair amount of literature from antiquity
~~~~~

because of my background in classics & ancient history, and so much of that's a delight to read. Homer, Aristophanes, Virgil, Catullus, Suetonius, and many other authors composed works that still enthral readers thousands of years later. But Mohammed's Quran is an ordeal. Possibly the worst book you'll ever read.

Its 114 surahs don't appear in any kind of thematic or chronological order. Instead, with a few exceptions such as the first surah being a short opening benediction, they're arranged in order of length, from longest to shortest. When you get to the 100s, the surahs are almost as short as the trovas I wrote for them. Arrangement aside, the surahs are supremely repetitive. As poeticised above, many of them go back to common material such as the story of Moses, sinners being tortured in hell, believers getting wine and magic sex slaves in heaven, and diatribes against anyone who doubts Mohammed's prophethood. Frankly, it's less a book and more a messy compilation of a politician's social media posts.

Perhaps that's why those of us from a Muslim background were raised to fetishise the book long before we actually read it. Molvis taught us to sound out Arabic, a language almost no one in my primarily Pakistani-origin British Muslim community understood, and they hit us when we mispronounced any of those uncomprehended words. Families took great pride in their children "reading the Quran" for the first time, meaning they'd sounded the entire thing out in Arabic. An utter waste of time. But effective in creating another generation that would mindlessly idolise the Quran and instinctively deflect any doubts and criticism they might encounter later in life.

That said, even if the Quran has no literary value, it has historical value. It provides our best insight into the historical Mohammed. The later Islamic tradition, the Hadith and so forth, provides a lot of biographical material about Mohammed, but none of it's historically reliable. It's just fanfic written in the centuries following his death. By contrast, if the Quran represents what Mohammed composed and preached and claimed was the word of Allah, it grants us glimpses into what kind of man he was. In short, he was a villain. He preached a supposed divine revelation that let him build a cult, rob and rape his enemies, and make himself into a de facto deity for the people he scammed, a man who could produce new words from Allah whenever he wanted something.

The Quran also has value because it makes Islam self-refuting.

Islam's central claim, the basis of Mohammed's alleged prophethood, is that the Quran's of extraterrestrial origin. Not just divinely inspired. The literal speech of an infallible deity, which an angel brought down piecemeal from heaven and relayed to Mohammed, word for word. This may make Islam the only major religion where its central claim can actually be tested. Because we have the Quran. We have the book of which Mohammed made that claim, which present-day Muslims continue to claim is Allah's literal, infallible speech. We can read it and see where Mohammed garbled Jewish and Christian stories, for example thinking Pharaoh of the Exodus story was a contemporary of Haman, when those characters actually appeared in Jewish stories set many centuries apart. We can see where Mohammed, like most people of his day, mistook the *Alexander Romance* for a genuine chronicle of the life and deeds of Alexander the Great, when in reality it's a historical fantasy novel that weaves magic and monsters into his exploits, and depicts him marching into Italy and subduing the Romans (something the real Alexander of Macedon certainly never did). And for those of us who dabble with poetry ourselves, we can see where Mohammed experimented with different poetic techniques, such as refrains.

Imagine a Christian gave you a bag of human bones and said, "These are the bones of Jesus. Proof he's our risen Lord!" That's essentially what

Muslims do when they brandish the Quran and claim it's the literal speech of an infallible deity. They present as proof of their religion something that actually refutes it.

No wonder Islam has to rely on blasphemy laws, mobs, and jihadist violence.

About the Author

Ibrahim S. Amin was educated at the Manchester Grammar School, the University of Newcastle, and the University of Manchester. He wallowed in education for as long as he could, earning his PhD in Classics & Ancient History. At that point he ran out of excuses and joined the real world — where he now writes to support his unhealthy takeaway addiction.

His previous books are:

The Monster Hunter's Handbook: The Ultimate Guide to Saving Mankind from Vampires, Zombies, Hellhounds, and Other Mythical Beasts

Jihad Squad

Clara Mandrake's Monster

Gorgon Street Girls

Apostasy, Blasphemy, Absurdity: A Poetry Chapbook

Fantasy, Fairies, Franiards: A Poetry Chapbook

Horrors, Terrors, Errors: A Poetry Chapbook

Fantasy, Mythology, Larceny: A Poetry Chapbook